ONE DIRECTION
TEST YOUR SUPER-FAN STATUS

Written by Jim Maloney and Jen Wainwright
Cover design by Zoe Quayle
Design by Barbara Ward
Edited by Jo Strange and Hannah Cohen

Picture Acknowledgements:

Front cover: John Marshall/AP/Press Association Images

Pages 1, 3, 4, 5: © Press Association Images
Page 2: Matt Baron/BEI/Rex Features
Pages 6–7: Erik Pendzich/Rex Features
Page 8: Dave Hogan/Getty Images

First edition for North America published in 2012
by Barron's Educational Series, Inc.

First published in Great Britain in 2012 by Buster Books,
an imprint of Michael O'Mara Books Limited,
9 Lion Yard, Tremadoc Road, London SW4 7NQ
www.mombooks.com/busterbooks

All inquiries should be addressed to:
Barron's Educational Series, Inc.
250 Wireless Boulevard
Hauppauge, NY 11788
www.barronseduc.com

PLEASE NOTE: This book is not affiliated with
or endorsed by One Direction or any of their
publishers or licensees.

ISBN-13: 978-1-4380-0201-9

Library of Congress Control No.: 2012935353

Date of Manufacture: April 2012
Manufactured by: Bind-Rite, Robbinsville, New Jersey

Printed in the United States of America
9 8 7 6 5 4 3 2

ONE DIRECTION

TEST YOUR SUPER-FAN STATUS

BARRON'S

CONTENTS

ABOUT THIS BOOK

Harry   Liam   Louis   Niall   Zayn

You pore over every performance and podcast, follow their tweets, plaster pictures of the fab five on your bedroom walls, and feel oh-so-proud as their album storms to the number one spot and breaks records. You're definitely a fan...but are you a SUPER-FAN?

Now's your chance to find out. Test your One Direction trivia knowledge, take on tons of cool quizzes and solve puzzles, crosswords, and wordsearches. Let your imagination run wild with incredible stories to fill in, then find out which band member you're destined to spend the perfect day with.

Are you ready for the challenge? If so, grab a pen and follow the instructions at the top of each page—you can check your answers on pages 91 to 95. Be ready to get clued up on the coolest boy band ever and discover what sort of One Direction fan you really are.

R U THEIR NO. 1 FAN?

So you think you know all about the One Direction boys? Take this quiz to see just how big a fan you really are. You can check your answers on page 91.

1. Who is the youngest member of the band?

    a. Niall
    b. Louis
    c. Harry

2. Which role did Louis play in his school production of *Grease*?

    a. Teen Angel
    b. Danny Zuko
    c. Kenickie

3. At age four, who sang "Let Me Entertain You" on stage at a vacation resort?

    a. Liam
    b. Zayn
    c. Niall

4. Which band was Harry in before he joined One Direction?

a. White Lightning
b. White Eskimo
c. White Seagull

5. Who had previously auditioned for British *X Factor* in 2008?

a. Louis
b. Harry
c. Liam

6. What did Harry say is his hidden talent?

a. Juggling
b. Making balloon animals
c. Card tricks

7. What did Liam say his super power would be?

a. He'd be invisible
b. He'd be able to fly
c. He'd have super strength

8. Who said their ideal job besides singing would be to work on a farm?

a. Zayn
b. Louis
c. Niall

9. Which subject did Harry say he was interested in studying at college?

a. Law
b. Psychology
c. Astrophysics

10. Which soccer player bought the boys tickets to watch England play France in London's Wembley stadium?
- **a.** Steven Gerrard
- **b.** Rio Ferdinand
- **c.** Wayne Rooney

11. At whose concert did Liam twist his ankle, while tripping backstage?
- **a.** Rihanna's
- **b.** Tinie Tempah's
- **c.** Lady Gaga's

12. Who did Harry say is his biggest pop idol?
- **a.** Elvis Presley
- **b.** Robbie Williams
- **c.** Justin Bieber

13. Which musical instrument can Niall play?
- **a.** Guitar
- **b.** Drums
- **c.** Piano

14. According to the others, which band member spends longest in front of the mirror?
- **a.** Niall
- **b.** Liam
- **c.** Zayn

15. What did Louis describe Harry as?
- **a.** The Know-It-All
- **b.** The Flirt
- **c.** The Comedian

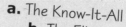

THE FACT FACTOR:

♡ HARRY ♡

Only four of these five statements about *HARRY STYLES* are true. Put a check in the circle beside each statement that you think is true, and a cross if it's a lie.

1. Harry is from Cheshire, England. ◯

2. Harry's hair isn't naturally curly. He curls it with a curling iron. ◯

3. When he auditioned for England's *X Factor*, Harry had a Saturday job in a bakery. ◯

4. Harry's favorite vegetable is sweet corn. ◯

5. Harry's favorite song is John Mayer's cover of "Free Fallin." ◯

Answers on page 91.

ALL DIRECTIONS

Just for a moment, forget about "one" direction and think all directions instead. Each of the words below is connected to the wonderful world of One Direction. Take a look at the grid on the opposite page and see if you can find them. The words appear in all directions—upwards, downwards, across columns, diagonally, or back to front. Check page 91 for the answers.

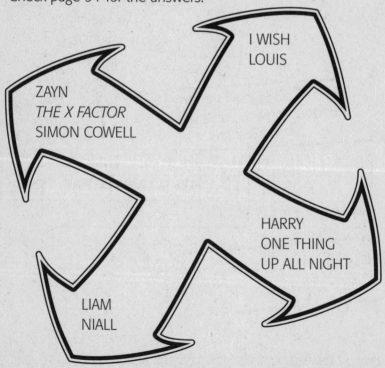

I WISH
LOUIS

ZAYN
THE X FACTOR
SIMON COWELL

HARRY
ONE THING
UP ALL NIGHT

LIAM
NIALL

T	A	D	S	H	S	O	R	B	S	G	S	A	H	C
T	F	A	C	X	L	L	Y	M	A	O	D	R	A	L
H	H	I	A	Z	E	L	H	A	X	O	E	F	R	L
E	R	U	F	Y	E	H	S	O	U	R	N	W	R	E
X	S	Y	P	P	D	G	I	E	H	Y	A	E	Y	W
F	O	C	E	A	M	R	W	F	A	E	Q	S	W	O
A	U	S	L	D	L	I	I	Z	G	F	U	A	P	C
C	P	A	D	A	V	L	E	S	K	H	H	L	A	N
T	G	N	I	H	T	E	N	O	W	J	G	L	B	O
O	O	B	T	K	O	K	U	I	O	W	D	S	C	M
R	N	E	G	F	L	Y	T	H	G	X	E	I	D	I
F	I	F	Z	Q	H	Z	H	Y	P	H	E	U	L	S
D	A	X	S	L	I	A	M	R	L	N	T	O	O	E
A	L	R	A	C	L	I	U	K	M	O	M	L	Y	T
J	L	S	T	O	U	P	P	N	A	D	U	G	Z	A

11

MEMORY GAMES

There's no doubt that the boys have shot to superstardom, but their true super-fans will always remember where they started. Test your memory with this British *X Factor* quiz, then turn to page 91 to see how you did.

1. What upbeat song did the boys sing for American Anthems week?

Answer ....

2. Name the other three group acts mentored by Simon in 2010.

Answer ....

....

....

3. After watching him perform his solo audition, *X Factor* judge, Louis Walsh said, "You are so young, I don't think you have enough experience or confidence yet." Who was Louis talking about?

Answer ....

4. Who said, "You are a boy band doing exactly what a boy band should do."

Answer ....

5. During Guilty Pleasures week, which judge confessed to the boys, "You're my guilty pleasure!"

Answer ....

6. What was the song that Harry first sang in front of the judges as a solo artist?

Answer ....

7. Who auditioned as a solo singer for Simon and was told, "I think you're unprepared. You came with the wrong song, you're not as good as you thought you were, but I still like you."

Answer ....

8. Before Simon gave him a pep talk, who refused to dance at boot camp?

Answer ....

9. What song did the boys sing for Halloween week?

Answer ....

10. After they sang the Beatles song, "All You Need Is Love," who said, "It's good to see the Fab Five singing the Fab Four!"

Answer ....

11. Who came down with stage fright during backstage rehearsals for Heroes week?

Answer ....

12. Who said of the boys, "I can't even cope with how cute you are!"

Answer ....

VIP TICKET

Imagine you've won a competition for a VIP ticket that lets you and your BFF spend a day with One Direction. What would you do? Where would you go? Fill in the gaps in the story below to find out. You can use the ideas in parentheses to help you, or make it up as you go along. Whatever happens, enjoy your VIP status while it lasts…

A huge limo arrives at your house. All the neighbors watch as the chauffeur opens the door and you and _____ *(your BFF's name)* step inside, looking like cool A-list stars.

"_____" *(This is the life!/I was born for luxury,,/It's a bit embarrassing!)* you say.

As the limo drives off, the chauffeur informs you that there is a TV and a stereo in the back, plus loads of tasty treats, and that you should help yourself.

"What a shame it's only an hour's drive. There's so much to do!" your friend says. You want a drink, and help yourself to _____ *(a fizzy drink/a milkshake/a glass of freshly squeezed juice)* Hmm, some music perhaps? Your friend puts on _____ *(your fave album)* and you both lounge back in the white leather seats.

Looking out of the tinted windows, it's fun to see all the looks you are getting from passersby. Ha! You can see them, but they can't see you—awesome!

To your amusement, you see your friends
_____ and _____
(their names). They are staring at the limo as if a celebrity is passing by. You press a button to lower the window and wave at them. Their jaws drop as they see you. Laughing, you shout,
"_____" *(I did tell you I was a star./Would you like my autograph?/Sorry, no photos!)*

You snack on some _____
(chips/sandwiches/cake) to calm your nerves. OMG...you are about to meet One Direction! The five-star journey soon comes to an end and the limo pulls up outside an expensive-looking apartment building.

You walk towards the apartment building. Your friend is speechless for once. You buzz the intercom and a voice calls you inside. After walking up the carpeted stairs, you enter another door and—gulp!—there they are.

Harry is lying on the bed watching TV, Liam is
_____, Louis is _____, and Zayn is _____ .

"You're here!" they shout, as if you are real-life VIPs.
"Let's _____ "

(have some fun./go crazy!/have a day to remember.)

Niall emerges from the other room and greets you
with a high-five. "How do you feel about going
_____?" *(roller-skating/
go-karting/rock climbing)* he says.

"Sounds amazing," you reply, then you all climb into the
back of the limo and set off.

Wow! What a day this is turning out to be. You had so
much fun at the _____ *(roller rink/
go-kart track/rock wall).* _____
(member of One Direction) congratulated you when you
were the first to _____ .

After so much fun and excitement, it's time to relax
over lunch. Niall suggests _____
(burgers and fries/pizza/grilled cheese sandwiches), but he
allows you to decide. You choose _____ .

During lunch you get the chance to ask the boys all
about themselves. Your friend asks _____
(member of One Direction) what his fave
_____ *(food/song/TV show)*
is. "_____ ," he replies.

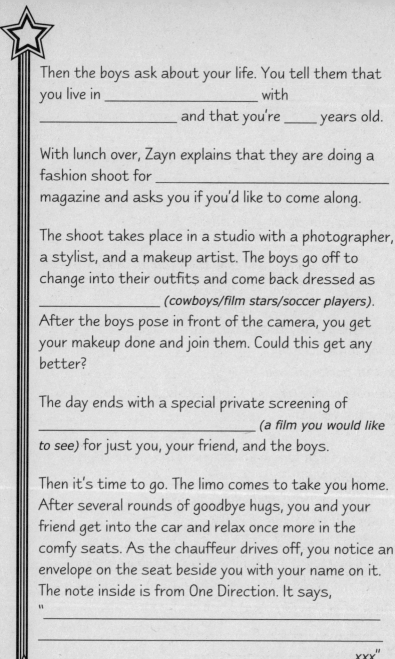

Then the boys ask about your life. You tell them that you live in _____ with _____ and that you're _____ years old.

With lunch over, Zayn explains that they are doing a fashion shoot for _____ magazine and asks you if you'd like to come along.

The shoot takes place in a studio with a photographer, a stylist, and a makeup artist. The boys go off to change into their outfits and come back dressed as _____ *(cowboys/film stars/soccer players)*. After the boys pose in front of the camera, you get your makeup done and join them. Could this get any better?

The day ends with a special private screening of _____ *(a film you would like to see)* for just you, your friend, and the boys.

Then it's time to go. The limo comes to take you home. After several rounds of goodbye hugs, you and your friend get into the car and relax once more in the comfy seats. As the chauffeur drives off, you notice an envelope on the seat beside you with your name on it. The note inside is from One Direction. It says,

"_____
_____
_____ *xxx*"

SECRET CRUSHES

Those gorgeous One Direction boys make plenty of their fans go weak in the knees, but now it's time to find out who makes them go a little starry-eyed and dreamy.

Read the following quotes and decide which of the boys said each one. Write your answers on the lines provided. Turn to page 91 when you think you've figured it out.

1. "Being in Cheryl Cole's presence was intimidating because she's so hot!"

Who said it?...........................

2. "My celebrity crush has got to be Leona Lewis. Everyone who's on my Twitter knows that. I love Leona Lewis."

Who said it?...........................

19

3. "My first celebrity crush was Megan Fox after I saw her in the Transformers movie."

Who said it?...........................

4. "I've been in love with Frankie Sandford since I was about eight. I'd love to kiss her."

Who said it?...........................

5. "I'm a big fan of Janet Devlin. Amazing singer, Irish, and most of all cute!"

Who said it?...........................

6. "My first real crush was Louis Tomlinson. It's a mutual thing. We've discussed it."

Who said it?...........................

7. "Demi Lovato, she seems like a really nice girl."

Who said it?...........................

LUCKY NUMBERS

You know that you're the number one fan of these five boys, but are you ready to play the numbers game? Read the statements below and match them with the correct numbers. Answers are on page 92.

1. Tracks on "Up All Night": ....

2. Highest singles chart position reached: ....

3. Minutes in which their tour of Australia and New Zealand sold out: ....

4. Week of *The X Factor* live shows the boys got to: ....

5. Age Liam was when he first auditioned for *The X Factor*: ....

6. 1D boys with the star sign Virgo: ....

WHAT ARE THE CHANCES?

TRUE OR FALSE TEST

Read these statements about One Direction, then decide if they are true or false. Check the circles to mark your answers, taking your best guess if you're not sure—the chances are 50/50 you'll guess right, so why not give it a try? Turn to page 92 to find out how you did.

---

1. Harry supports Manchester United Soccer Club.

True ○
False ○

---

2. Simon Cowell said the band reminded him of five Beatles.

True ○
False ○

---

3. Niall once had a pet hamster he called Jaws.

True ○
False ○

4. The furthest Louis has traveled from home is Marbella, Spain.

True ⭘
False ⭘

5. Zayn has three sisters.

True ⭘
False ⭘

6. Harry was 11 when he had his first kiss.

True ⭘
False ⭘

7. Zayn liked playing Scrabble in *The X Factor* house.

True ⭘
False ⭘

8. Louis has a collection of rubber ducks at home.

True ⭘
False ⭘

9. Simon Cowell forgot Zayn's name and called him Olly.

True ⭘
False ⭘

10. Liam can count up to one hundred in Swahili.

True ⭘
False ⭘

11. The Script is one of Niall's fave bands.

True ◯
False ◯

12. Zayn's fave TV show is *Antiques Roadshow*.

True ◯
False ◯

13. Harry left a banana peel in the bathtub of *The X Factor* house.

True ◯
False ◯

14. Louis once felt "seasick" in the bathtub.

True ◯
False ◯

15. British *X Factor* diva Cher Lloyd beat Harry at arm wrestling.

True ◯
False ◯

Feeling confident? Here's a last-minute hint . . .
There were six true statements and nine false statements. Go back and check you have the right number of each.

TWEET TWEET

The boys are big tweeters on the social networking site Twitter. Can you guess which band member posted these tweets? Write your answer at the bottom of the page then check page 92 to see if you guessed correctly.

I would just like to thank every single one of you who bought a ticket to come and see us on tour. We really did have an amazing time :)

Mcdonalds breakfast wrap get in my mouth.

Public apology for being late for rehearsals. :)

Feeling very very happy :)

Today is a good day :) and just found out What Makes You Beautiful has over 50,000,000 views on YouTube. Massive thank you to everyone :)

The mystery tweeter is ...

Answer...........................

IN THE STARS

Discover what your star sign says about you and then see which band member you'd spend your perfect day with.

AQUARIUS (January 21st–February 19th)

Personality Traits: honest, loyal, inventive
Likes: acting, trying new things, being active
Dislikes: boredom, not being able to be creative
Your Ideal Day: Talking, music, books, and life in general with Zayn. Later, you'd put your creative minds to work by writing a new hit song together. Quick, somebody get Simon Cowell on the phone!

PISCES (February 20th–March 20th)

Personality Traits: trustworthy, creative, emotional
Likes: reading, painting, drawing, writing
Dislikes: being the center of attention, parties
Your Ideal Day: You'd enjoy a good heart-to-heart with Liam, discussing what you both want from life while on a gondola in Venice. Come sunset, you enjoy the views in not-at-all-awkward silence. Bliss!

ARIES (March 21st–April 20th)

Personality Traits: spontaneous, ambitious, energetic
Likes: adventure, meeting new people, outdoor sports
Dislikes: staying at home, organization, board games
Your Ideal Day: For you, it's a trip to the circus with Louis. You two don't miss a second of fun and you're joking around like a couple of clowns on the way home.

TAURUS (April 21st–May 21st)

Personality Traits: sympathetic, dependable, practical
Likes: helping others, being outside, old friends, making things
Dislikes: unreliable people, feeling out of control
Your Ideal Day: A lazy afternoon spent sitting by a lake with Harry, skimming stones and making sketches of the beautiful surroundings, suits you perfectly. Throw in a delicious homemade picnic and you're truly in heaven.

GEMINI (May 22nd–June 21st)

Personality Traits: adaptable, imaginative, witty
Likes: trying new experiences, lively conversation
Dislikes: being alone, not knowing the latest gossip
Your Ideal Day: Always looking to try something new, you would rent a karaoke booth with Niall. You'd have an awesome time trying on all the different wigs and arguing over which cheesy tune to sing next.

CANCER (June 22nd–July 23rd)

Personality Traits: protective, independent, sensitive
Likes: being at home, history, cooking
Dislikes: disorganization, being let down by others
Your Ideal Day: Being a sensitive guy, Harry will bring out the nurturing side in you as you both cook up a storm in the kitchen, creating a meal that any TV chef would be proud of. Harry insists on not following the recipe, and you go along with him—just this once.

LEO (July 24th–August 23rd)
Personality Traits: dynamic, self-assured, intuitive
Likes: luxury, being center stage, parties
Dislikes: having nothing to do, indecision, grumpiness
Your Ideal Day: It's got to be an adventurous activity course with Louis—canoeing, rock climbing, or perhaps even parachuting! Laid-back Louis is up for all of them, so he's leaving it up to you to choose. Better decide quickly, as he likes to get going.

VIRGO (August 24th–September 23rd)
Personality Traits: charming, easy-going, flexible
Likes: being helpful, making others laugh, new hobbies
Dislikes: stubborn people, selfishness, seriousness
Your Ideal Day: Niall surprises you with tickets to watch his favorite soccer team. It's cold at the match, so he lends you his scarf. It clashes with your outfit, but you couldn't care less because you're having so much fun. Later, it's back home for a meal with his family. Aww …

LIBRA (September 24th–October 23rd)
Personality Traits: understanding, caring, fair
Likes: harmony, being active, chilling out with friends
Dislikes: making decisions, competitive people
Your Ideal Day: You'd enjoy a day at the bowling alley with Harry and a few of your friends. Who has got the most strikes? You've no idea. No one is bothering to keep score because you're all having such a good time.

SCORPIO (October 24th–November 22nd)

Personality Traits: bold, determined, a bit mysterious
Likes: a good argument, keeping in touch, parties
Dislikes: boredom, being alone, showing feelings
Your Ideal Day: Get down and party with energetic Niall. There is nothing stopping you as you both show off your moves on the dance floor. Everyone else is wowed by how well-choreographed you two appear—are you sure you haven't been practicing?

SAGITTARIUS (November 23rd–December 21st)

Personality Traits: generous, lively, philosophical
Likes: traveling, sports, helping people
Dislikes: schedules, downbeat people, sharing problems
Your Ideal Day: Liam's decided you're going to get on the next train that leaves the station and see where you end up. Result—it's the beach! You spend the day playing in the arcades and munching on fries on the pier, ending the perfect day by catching a movie.

CAPRICORN (December 22nd–January 20th)

Personality Traits: organized, patient, down-to-earth
Likes: rules, sharing confidences, being nosey
Dislikes: injustice, shallow or inconsiderate people
Your Ideal Day: There's not much you enjoy more than hitting the stores with Zayn as your partner in crime. Today's a case of shop 'til you drop, then collapse into a cozy restaurant for a top-notch meal. You've spent a little too much, so it's on Zayn—phew!

TOTAL TRIVIA ?

It's all here—totally cool trivia about your fave five.
But as usual, you have to work for your reward.
How many questions will you get right? The answers
are revealed on page 92.

Which one of the boys said ...

1. "If I were a food I'd be a rogan josh because they're tasty."

Who said it?.....................

2. "I once set up loads of candles in a park for a girl I really liked, but she didn't come along as she was too scared of the dark!"

Who said it?.....................

3. "When I was about eight I had a dream that a giant Power Ranger was chasing me around."

Who said it?.....................

When asked, "What is the most loving and caring thing you would ever do for a girl?" who replied ...

?

4. "I would take a girl on a romantic vacation."

Who said it?......................

5. "I would write her a song."

Who said it?.....................

Time for some multiple choice ...

?

6. Harry said he could play which instrument?

a. Drums
b. Flute
c. Kazoo

7. Who did the boys draw a mustache on with marker while he was asleep?

a. Niall
b. Harry
c. Liam

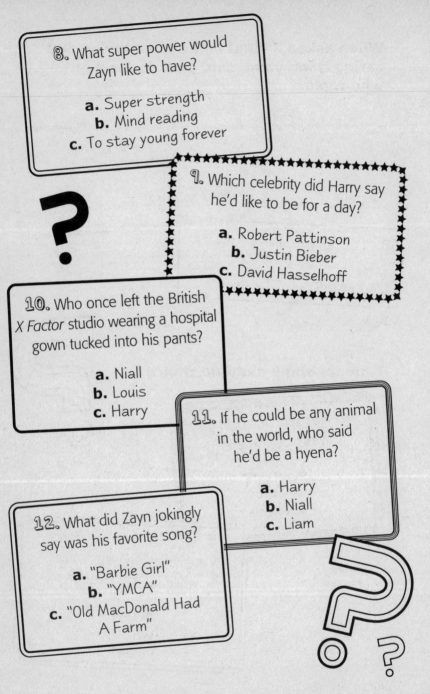

8. What super power would Zayn like to have?

a. Super strength
b. Mind reading
c. To stay young forever

9. Which celebrity did Harry say he'd like to be for a day?

a. Robert Pattinson
b. Justin Bieber
c. David Hasselhoff

10. Who once left the British *X Factor* studio wearing a hospital gown tucked into his pants?

a. Niall
b. Louis
c. Harry

11. If he could be any animal in the world, who said he'd be a hyena?

a. Harry
b. Niall
c. Liam

12. What did Zayn jokingly say was his favorite song?

a. "Barbie Girl"
b. "YMCA"
c. "Old MacDonald Had A Farm"

THE FACT FACTOR:
♡ LIAM ♡

Here are four facts and one fib about **LIAM PAYNE**. Put a check in the circle beside each statement that you think is true, and a cross if it's a lie.

1. Liam is from Wolverhampton, England. ○

2. Besides singing, his ideal job would be as a PE teacher. ○

3. Liam has a phobia of jelly. ○

4. Of all the celebrities in the world, he would most like to be British comedian Michael McIntyre. ○

5. He can play some guitar and piano. ○

Answers on page 92.

CRISSCROSSED

Read the clues below and see how quickly you can write your answers in the crossword grid on the opposite page. Check out the answers on page 92 when you're done.

Across

1. UK TV show *Red or*_____ where the boys performed their first single live (5)

3. Last name of the band's Irish member (5)

6. Name of the first single the boys released in 2012 (3, 5)

Down

2. This rival *X Factor* contestant has real swagger (4, 5)

3. The single the *X Factor* finalists released for charity (6)

4. The boys won one of these prestigious awards in February 2012 (4)

5. The December charity concert in London's 02 arena, where the band performed. "_____ Bell Ball" (6)

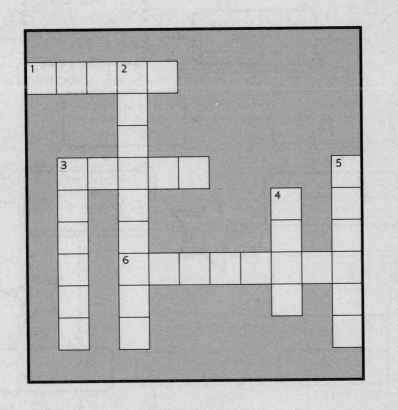

35

THE FLOW FACTOR
IT'S THE AUDITIONS ...

You will need: dice

Start
The X Factor auditions are coming to your town. What do you do?

Get some bandmates together, pronto!

When picking bandmates, what do you do?

Pick your best friend. It'll be fun to do it together.

Search far and wide for the best singers to give yourself the best chance.

Your best friend is out of tune. The judges give you the option to go solo. What do you do?

It's audition day. Roll the dice to find out what the judges think of you.

1, 2, or 3.

4, 5, or 6.

Stick with your friend out of loyalty.

Congratulations, you made it to boot camp! Your confidence is soaring—whoop whoop!

What? *Nooooo!* You didn't make it. You sob your heart out on live television and resolve to try again next year.

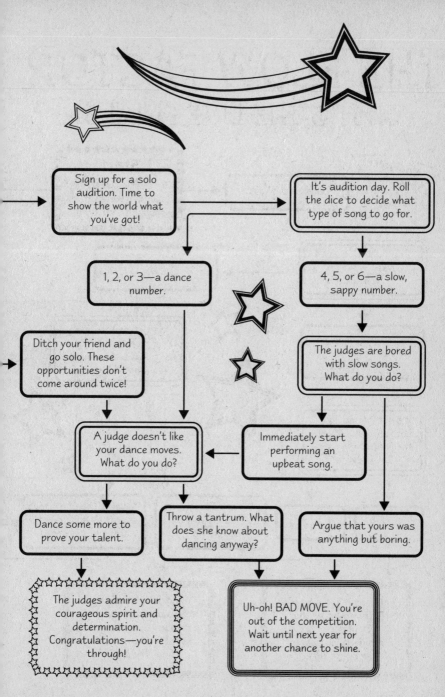

Sign up for a solo audition. Time to show the world what you've got!

It's audition day. Roll the dice to decide what type of song to go for.

1, 2, or 3—a dance number.

4, 5, or 6—a slow, sappy number.

Ditch your friend and go solo. These opportunities don't come around twice!

The judges are bored with slow songs. What do you do?

A judge doesn't like your dance moves. What do you do?

Immediately start performing an upbeat song.

Dance some more to prove your talent.

Throw a tantrum. What does she know about dancing anyway?

Argue that yours was anything but boring.

The judges admire your courageous spirit and determination. Congratulations—you're through!

Uh-oh! BAD MOVE. You're out of the competition. Wait until next year for another chance to shine.

THE FLOW FACTOR
... IT'S THE LIVE FINALS!

You will need: dice

Start
It's Beatles Week this Saturday. What do you choose to perform?

"Twist and Shout"

One judge is in a bad mood. What do you do?

Try to cheer them up by being playful.

Concentrate on pleasing another judge, who you know likes you.

It's the quarter final. Your mentor's picked a song that's all wrong for you. What do you do?

It's not looking good, but you could still be the judges' wild card. Roll the dice.

1, 2, or 3.

4, 5, or 6.

Cry a little during your performance.

Pull off the performance regardless and bring the crowd to their feet.

Oh dear! The dream is truly over for you. You're out of the competition. Better luck next time!

You did something right because you made it through the semis, but were knocked out in the final. The agony!

38

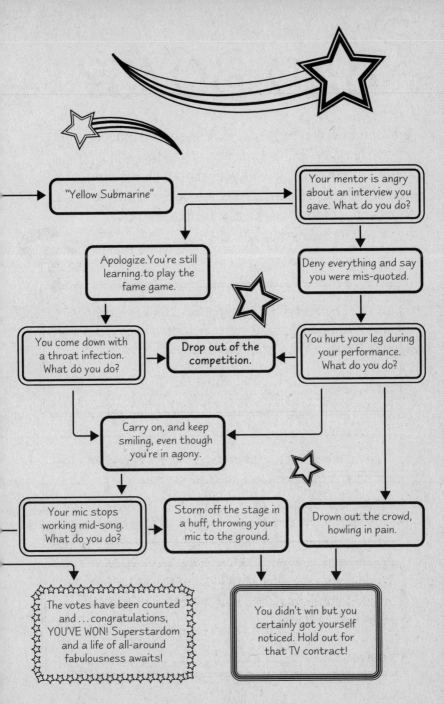

"Yellow Submarine"

Your mentor is angry about an interview you gave. What do you do?

Apologize. You're still learning.to play the fame game.

Deny everything and say you were mis-quoted.

You come down with a throat infection. What do you do?

Drop out of the competition.

You hurt your leg during your performance. What do you do?

Carry on, and keep smiling, even though you're in agony.

Your mic stops working mid-song. What do you do?

Storm off the stage in a huff, throwing your mic to the ground.

Drown out the crowd, howling in pain.

The votes have been counted and...congratulations, YOU'VE WON! Superstardom and a life of all-around fabulousness awaits!

You didn't win but you certainly got yourself noticed. Hold out for that TV contract!

39

BAD BOYS?

The One Direction boys may look sweet and innocent—*especially* Harry—but boys will be boys. High spirits, harmless pranks, call it what you will, but their moms wouldn't like it. Can you answer the questions below about some of their less-pleasant antics? You can check your answers on page 93.

1. The boys don't just play pranks on each other. Which famously scary music maestro received some prank phone calls from the 1D boys?

Answer ....

2. In a video diary, who had his mouth taped up with masking tape to make him stay quiet?

Answer ....

3. While on tour, one of the boys shaved his initials into his bandmate's leg hair! Which mischievous member did this?

Answer ....

4. Who said "Louis regularly breaks into my room and throws buckets of water over me when I'm sleeping."

Answer ....

5. Which of the band was dared by the others to drink a mixture of mustard, ketchup, soda, and milkshake? Mmm, tasty!

Answer ....

6. Which one of the five do they all agree is the laziest?

Answer ....

7. Finally, which mischievous band member are the following *X Factor* contestants all talking about?

Matt Cardle: "He's the cheekiest* person I've ever met in my life. But got to love him."
Mary Byrne: "He's the cheekiest of the whole group. He does naughty things. He's just mad."
Cher Lloyd: "He's cheeky to everybody."

Answer ....

cheeky is a British word used to describe someone who is bold, brazen, and in-your-face.

TWEET TWEET

There is a mystery Twitter-tweeter on the loose. Can you guess which band member posted the following tweets? Write your answer at the bottom of the page then check page 93 to see if your powers of detection are strong!

"peace and love make the world go round :)
goodnight peeps :) x"

"Btw can I apologize for my spelling .. I just do it to make all the words fit into a tweet promise :D"

"So remember when I said I was having an early night .. I changed my mind :) x"

"Get on with life, because life gets on without you x"

":) soo just done the fitting for the show some dapper clothes flying about :D x"

The mystery tweeter is ...

Answer...............................

THE FACT FACTOR:
♡ NIALL ♡

Here are four facts and one fib about NIALL HORAN.
Put a check in the circle beside each statement that you
think is true and a cross if it's a lie.

1. Niall's dad said he always wanted to be a soccer player when he was younger. ○

2. Niall has never had a job. ○

3. Niall is an avid supporter of Derby County Soccer Club. ○

4. Niall had planned to go to college to learn how to be a sound engineer. ○

5. Niall's fave boy band is Irish group Westlife. ○

Answers on page 93.

IT'S ALL TALK!

Tons of celebrities have had something to say about One Direction, but the boys have had quite a bit to say for themselves, too! Read the five quotes on these pages and decide which band member said what. Mark your answers by linking each quote number to the right band member on the opposite page. Turn to page 93 to see if you guessed right.

Which one of the boys said ...

1. "We've all wanted the same thing from the start, so I came up with the name One Direction."

2. "Being in LA is such a different lifestyle. It's really fast-paced. I mean, the furthest place I'd ever been before *The X Factor* was Birmingham."*

---

*Birmingham, England, is 88 miles from this member's hometown.

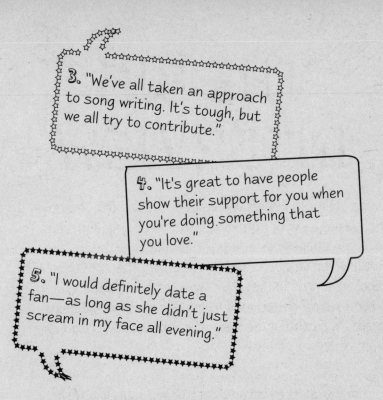

3. "We've all taken an approach to song writing. It's tough, but we all try to contribute."

4. "It's great to have people show their support for you when you're doing something that you love."

5. "I would definitely date a fan—as long as she didn't just scream in my face all evening."

Draw lines to link each quote number to who you think said them. The first one has been done for you.

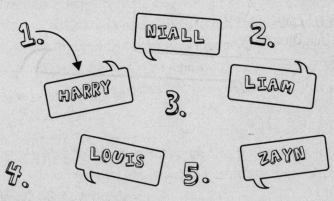

1. → HARRY

NIALL

2.

3.

LIAM

LOUIS

4.

5.

ZAYN

THE BIG INTERVIEW

Wow! This is the news you've been waiting for. The boys are playing in your hometown and, as a mega-fan, your local newspaper has asked you to interview them. But first you've got to track them down. The editor has received a tip that they are staying at the Hilltop Hotel, so you set off determined to find them. Fill in the blank spaces with one of the suggested options or go wild and write whatever you like.

You arrive at the Hilltop Hotel, heart pounding with excitement, but trying to keep a professional cool. Walking boldly through the doors, you approach the receptionist and tell her you are a journalist and ask if One Direction are staying at the hotel. The receptionist snootily replies that she is not allowed to comment, so you wander off and sit down by a window, wondering what tactic to try next.

It's then that you notice a _____
(limousine/crowd gathering/familiar face) outside in the parking lot. You rush outside and bump into
_____ (Niall Horan/Simon Cowell/
Louis Tomlinson) making his way into the hotel lobby.

After blushing A LOT and stumbling through an apology, you follow him back into the hotel. You are about to introduce yourself, when the receptionist looks angrily at you and points towards the door.

Back outside you look around, wondering what to do next. The newspaper isn't going to be happy if you don't get your interview, and you aren't going to be happy if you don't get to meet your dream band.

Just then you hear _____ (a whistle/a shout/the sound of singing) coming from above you. You look up and there, to your amazement, is _____ (Louis Tomlinson/Niall Horan), waving out of a hotel room window. Yes!

You wave back excitedly, but then realize that he is waving to _____ (Harry Styles/Zayn Malik/Liam Payne), who is making his way towards the entrance, surrounded by hulking bodyguards.

You watch as they disappear inside. You begin to think that you have missed your chance. To make matters worse, the scary receptionist appears again and angrily tells you to leave the premises.

You find a bench in the garden area and slump down. It's probably time to call the newspaper editor to say that you have failed. You were sure you could do the job but with your bad luck you wonder whether you've got what it takes to be a journalist.

Just then, a figure approaches and says, "_____ _____ "
(Cheer up./What's the matter?/Is this seat taken?)

Without looking up, you mumble, "_____ , "
(I'm fine/Sure/I'm just going) and hope they go away.

Out of the corner of your eye you see the person staring at you. Irritated, you turn towards them, and then gasp suddenly. No way, it's _____
(Louis/Niall/Harry/Liam/Zayn)!

He asks if he can do anything to help put a smile on your face. You blurt out your problem at a million miles an hour. He just smiles, tells you to relax, and says,
"_____ "
(Interview me now./Come and meet the boys!)

You can't believe it, you did get lucky after all! The newspaper is so impressed with your exclusive interview that they offer you more reporting work. This is great news and you're sure you can handle more exclusive meetings with your fave boy band. Success!

Now turn to page 49 and write up your dream newspaper interview with One Direction.

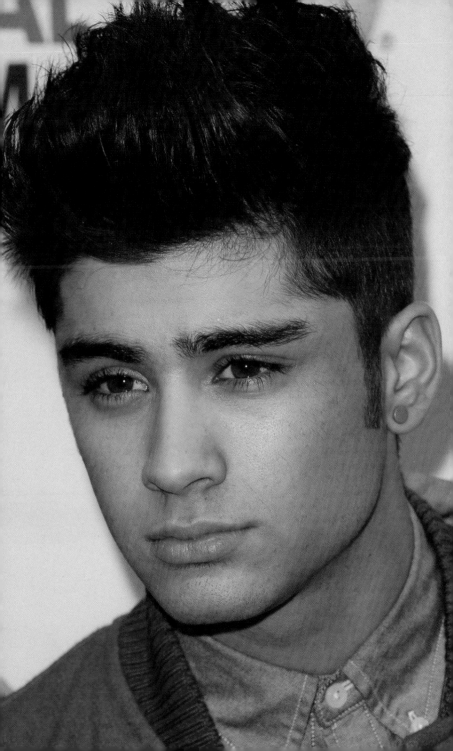

I ♥ ONE DIRECTION

SPOT THE DIFFERENCE

There are six differences between these two pictures. Can you spot them? Check your answers on page 93.

EXCLUSIVE INTERVIEW
WITH ONE DIRECTION

By _____
(Write your name.)

NAUGHTY OR NICE?

They became pals right from the moment that Simon Cowell suggested they form a group. But, good friends as they are, not all their comments about each other are flattering. Read the comments below and check off whether you think they are being naughty or nice!

LIAM: "I'd like to be Niall for the day because he finds everything 'ABSOLUTELY AMAZING'."

NAUGHTY ◯   ◯ NICE

ZAYN: "I'd like to be Louis for the day because he is just so hilarious."

NAUGHTY ◯   ◯ NICE

LOUIS: "Living in the contestants' house it's good to be in a group because if you ever have any problems or, on the flipside, if you're up for a laugh, you've got four other lads to turn to."

NAUGHTY ◯   ◯ NICE

ZAYN: "Niall farts. He farts all the time."

NAUGHTY ⃝   ⃝ NICE

LOUIS: "Harry's the flirt. Zayn is vain."

NAUGHTY ⃝   ⃝ NICE

When Zayn missed rehearsals for The X Factor semi-finals:

LIAM: "I miss Zaynnnn :(I love ya man."

NAUGHTY ⃝   ⃝ NICE

When asked why Harry gets so much attention from girls:

LIAM: "It's the curly hair…"

ZAYN: "Yeah, that's where his power is."

NAUGHTY ⃝   ⃝ NICE

Posting a photo on Twitter of his sleeping bandmates:

HARRY: "Look who fell asleep in the car ;) hahaha!!"

NAUGHTY ⃝   ⃝ NICE

Whose comments are the nicest?

Answer ....

WHICH DIRECTION?

No matter how you look at it—up, down, across, back to front and even diagonally—every word below can be associated with One Direction. Can you find the ten words below hidden on the opposite page? The answers are on page 93.

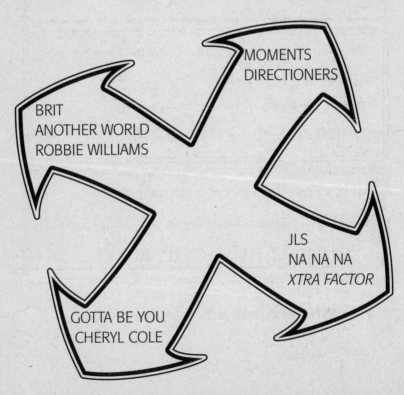

MOMENTS
DIRECTIONERS

BRIT
ANOTHER WORLD
ROBBIE WILLIAMS

JLS
NA NA NA
XTRA FACTOR

GOTTA BE YOU
CHERYL COLE

A	W	L	C	X	T	R	A	F	A	C	T	O	R	A
S	S	M	A	I	L	L	I	W	E	I	B	B	O	R
F	B	R	I	T	C	D	A	P	I	C	H	N	O	G
S	X	D	D	E	A	V	C	N	G	U	L	L	J	A
C	T	I	U	O	Y	E	B	A	T	T	O	G	N	M
H	R	R	A	C	B	F	W	N	L	E	F	O	X	G
E	O	E	K	P	U	H	Y	A	S	O	T	Y	I	P
R	P	C	I	K	S	T	C	N	N	H	O	Y	M	L
Y	O	T	S	W	O	P	E	A	E	B	K	Y	S	G
L	O	I	S	F	H	T	I	R	A	F	W	I	L	M
C	N	O	C	E	S	B	W	Q	L	Y	T	H	J	I
O	W	N	E	G	C	O	O	U	G	H	L	L	T	X
L	T	E	B	P	R	R	A	I	D	O	E	D	I	V
E	F	R	A	L	T	S	T	N	E	M	O	M	L	F
A	L	S	D	T	O	W	G	H	O	O	Y	P	A	O

CELEB FACTOR

Everyone who's anyone loves One Direction. Can you match the quotes to the celebrities who said them? The celebrities are listed at the bottom of the opposite page. The good news is that there are some little clues to help you out. The bad news? To make it trickier, there are more celebrities than quotes! Turn to page 94 for the answers.

---

1. "One Direction is the strongest boy band *The X Factor's* ever had."

Clue: Westlife member. Answer ....

---

2. "The girls are going to go crazy for these boys. It's like five Justin Biebers."

Clue: "Climbed" to the top. Answer ....

---

3. "I think Zayn is beautiful. He's perfection!"

Clue: A little muffin. Answer ....

54

4. "They're like our little brothers."

Clue: He's glad you came. Answer.....................................

5. "I just met One Direction and they were such gentlemen. I was very impressed."

Clue: A magical star. Answer ....

6. "I have a huge soft spot for those boys."

Clue: Impartial? Answer ....

7. "They'll be huge if they stay together."

Clue: Radioactive? Answer ....

8. "They are like five Mark Owens."

Clue: Making "progress." Answer ....

SO WHO SAID WHAT?

NATHAN SYKES

DERMOT O'LEARY

DANNY JONES

LEIGH-ANNE PINNOCK

FRANKIE SANDFORD

WILL.I.AM

JOE McELDERRY

KIMBERLEY WALSH

AGGRO SANTOS

EMMA WATSON

ROBBIE WILLIAMS

MARK FEEHILY

55

TOUR TIME

One Direction are due to kick off their massive tour tonight, but a clumsy typist has made a mess of the paperwork, getting all the letters mixed up.

Can you help the band out and unscramble the names below to see which songs the boys will be belting out on stage tonight?

If you get stuck, you can find the answers on page 94.

COVERS

A. BOONDY WONKS

....

B. LNOY RGIL NI HET DROLW

....

C. NORT

....

D. UYRO GNSO

....

1. KTNEA

....

2. TATOG EB UYO

....

3. TWAH KMAES UOY FLTEBUAIU

....

4. PU LLA THING

....

5. ELTL EM A IEL

....

6. I DHULSO VHAE SKIDSE UYO

....

7. NEO HGNIT

....

8. VASE YUO NOHGITT

....

TWEET TWEET

Time for some Twitter fun! Who do you think posted the following tweets on Twitter? Write your answer at the bottom of the page, then check page 94 to see if you were right.

Was that tired this morning, for the first time since i was like 4 , i tripped over my trouser leg as i was gettin into them! #floor

WOW! just found out that "up all night" is the biggest debut album of the year! We owe this all to you guys! Once again, thank you!

watchin a movie on the bus...chillin before next show

michael buble is my hero! look at the guy!

You guys have been incredible on this tour ! Soo loud and out in force! Love you all, not for a second does your support come unnoticed ! Xx

The mystery tweeter is ...

Answer.............................

THE FACT FACTOR:
♡ LOUIS ♡

Here are four facts and one fib about **LOUIS TOMLINSON**. Put a check in the circle beside each statement that you think is true, and a cross if you think it's a lie.

1. Louis is from Doncaster, England. ◯

2. Louis described his kiss on the cheek from Cheryl Cole as the best moment in his life. ◯

3. He can play a little bit of piano. ◯

4. His great-grandmother competed in the javelin at the 1936 Olympic Games. ◯

5. He says he likes girls who eat carrots! ◯

Answers on page 94.

FOREVER OR A DAY?

Try this fun quiz, then turn to page 94 to discover just what kind of One Direction fan you are. Are you a part-time fan, a loyal fan, or the ultimate, life-long fan?

1. Who is Liam's fave boy band?

    a. *NSYNC
    b. Boyzone
    c. Take That

2. What did Harry say would be his ideal job besides singing?

    a. Comedian
    b. Lawyer
    c. Hairdresser

3. What is Zayn's catchphrase?

    a. "Do you come here often?"
    b. "Haven't we met before?"
    c. "Vas happenin'?"

4. What super power would Louis most like to have?

a. To fly
b. X-ray vision
c. To freeze people

5. Which celebrity did Niall say he would most like to be for a day?

a. Ronan Keating
b. Justin Bieber
c. Michael Bublé

6. What did Louis say was his fave pick-up line?

a. You have the "X" factor
b. Up for a laugh?
c. Will you marry me?

7. Which band member most often sang the opening lines of One Direction's *X Factor* performances?

a. Zayn
b. Liam
c. Niall

8. Which song did Liam say he most enjoyed singing on *The X Factor*?

a. "Kids In America"
b. "Total Eclipse Of The Heart"
c. "Viva La Vida"

9. What qualities does Niall look for in a girl?

a. Cute with a good personality
b. Pretty and sweet
c. Fun and adventurous

10. What is Harry's idea of a perfect date?

a. A film with some popcorn
b. A romantic dinner
c. Ice-skating and a hot dog

11. Who said, "We couldn't imagine coming to America, let alone releasing our album here, so for us to be sitting at the top of the U.S. album charts is unbelievable."

a. Liam
b. Niall
c. Louis

12. Which celebrity would Zayn most like to be for a day?

a. Tinie Tempah
b. David Beckham
c. Lewis Hamilton

13. Who did Louis joke was his favorite "boy band?"

a. Girls Aloud
b. The Rolling Stones
c. Robbie Williams

14. Which soccer club does Niall support?

a. Manchester City
b. Newcastle United
c. Derby County

15. What color eyes does Liam most like in a girl?

a. Green
b. Blue
c. Brown

Don't forget to check page 94 to find out if you are One Direction's No.1 fan.

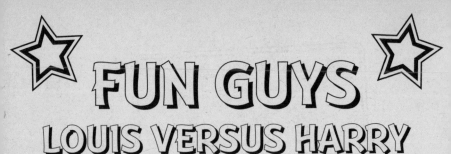

FUN GUYS
LOUIS VERSUS HARRY

The two jokers in the pack are Louis and Harry. Louis is loud, random and silly—Harry is ridiculous, sassy, and daring. But who is the funniest? You be the judge. Give each item a rating from one to five, according to how funny you think it is. Then add up both of the boys' scores to find out who is the biggest jokester.

LOUIS

RATING:

"Why did the mushroom go to the party? Because he was a fungi."

?/5

"I started to read the David Beckham book but my dog ate it. True story."

?/5

When asked, "If you were a food, what would type of food would you like to be?" Louis replied: "I think I'd just be a ruler."

?/5

HARRY

RATING:

"My favorite party trick is to wear nothing but a gold thong in the house. The Belle Amie girls say I prance around the house in it. I'd say it's more of a slow, gentle stroll."

From Harry's Twitter tweets: "Do you ever look in the mirror and think ... what wattage is my microwave?! :)"

"For Simon's birthday we got him a birthday card and taped $2.50 into it. That's 50¢ from each of us. He can buy whatever he wants with it."

Add up the total scores to see who you think is the funniest, Louis or Harry?

LOUIS   HARRY

....

BEST. DAY. EVER.

You have found out where One Direction will be shooting their new video—and it's not far from where you live. You and your friends are invited to go along and watch the filming—you can't believe your luck.

Complete the diary below, detailing your best day ever. You can use the words or guidelines in brackets to help you, or simply write whatever you like to create your dream day.

I couldn't believe it when I read _____
(in a magazine/in the newspaper/on the internet) that One Direction were filming their new video near where I live.

It's the best news ever. I call my BFFs
_____ and _____
(their names) to tell them. All of us were determined that we should go there and actually see them in the flesh.

We all have our own favorite band member. Mine is
_____ , while _____ likes _____
and _____ is a big fan of _____.

As the big day arrived, so did the big question—what to wear? Eventually I decided to wear my fave

_____ *(article of clothing)*, along with my _____ *(article of clothing)*, and my new _____ *(shoes/necklace/belt)*.

We set off on the bus and chatted excitedly all the way until it was time to get off. After a short walk, we saw lots of trailers, cars, and cameras ahead and ran towards them. We couldn't stop giggling.

A security guard was just about to stop us when Liam came out of his trailer and flashed us a brilliant smile. We were speechless. But he wasn't.

"_____"

(Come to watch the filming?/Are you cold?/Would you like a hot chocolate?) he asked.

"_____,"

I stammered. WOW.

Liam started showing us around and introduced us to Harry, Louis, and Niall. "Where's Zayn?" I asked, and the others laughed and said, "_____

_____"

(Putting on his makeup./Designing some clothes./Checking himself out in the mirror!)

Then Liam introduced us to the director of the video. He said they were just about to start filming. The One Direction boys took off their jackets and got ready to perform.

"Action!" shouted the director, as the backing track to their latest hit was played. The boys started to sing along, laughing and teasing each other at the same time. "Cut!" yelled the director. "Something's not right. We need more going on."

Silly Louis suggested they _____
_____
(paint themselves green/dress up as school girls/do some robot dancing).

While the other band members laughed at Louis, the director suddenly looked straight at us and asked if we would like to appear in the video. Was he joking? This was incredible! Too excited to be able to speak, we just managed to nod. It was a good job we'd planned our outfits well and we weren't having a bad hair day! Very soon we found ourselves _____ *(dancing/singing/cheering)* in the background as the boys did their stuff. It was _____ *(awesome/amazing/the best fun ever)*. Just wait till our other friends hear about this!

Afterwards, Liam said to us, "_____
_____ " *(That was great./*
Thank you so much./You should be in all our videos.)

He invited us into his trailer, where we relaxed with the
boys and got to ask each of them questions. I asked
_____ what his favorite meal was and he
told me it's _____ .
Then he asked me my fave memory and I explained
about the time when _____
_____
_____
_____
_____ .

At the end of our perfect day, we all said goodbye and
the boys said that they hoped they would see us again.
Just as we were leaving, _____ called me
back and gave me _____
_____
(his telephone number/tickets to their next concert/his shirt
to keep).

We made our way back home, hardly able to speak
because we were so amazed by what had happened.
Not in our wildest dreams did we expect it to be the
BEST. DAY. EVER.

SHHH ...!

Here are some surprising and embarrassing facts about the boys—some of which they might prefer you didn't know. Can you guess which cringe-worthy fact relates to which band member? Write a name below each fact, then turn to page 95 to reveal the answers.

1. He says his most embarrassing moment was when he split his trousers on stage during *The X Factor* tour. Cringe!

Guess who? ....

2. Nerves nearly stopped him from entering *The X Factor* until he got a good talking to from his mom.

Guess who? ....

3. He admits to talking in his sleep "all the time."

Guess who? ....

4. His first kiss was with a girl much taller than him so he stood on a brick before puckering up.

Guess who? ....

5. His mom came to the *X Factor* studio with cakes, sausage rolls, and apple slices.

Guess who? ....

EEW ...

6. *X Factor* contestant Wagner said this band member picked his nose and made snot balls.

Guess who? ....

7. He used to have a recurring dream in which he used to forget to put clothes on and go to school naked.

Guess who? ....

8. He admits his bad habit is snoring.

Guess who? ....

ERR ...?

9. If he could be a celebrity for a day he would most like to be Susan Boyle because "she is a good dancer."

Guess who? ....

WHAT WOULD YOU DO?

What would you do if you had the chance to spend some time with the boys? Take a look at the options below. All you have to do is check your preferred choice for each pair of options. But beware, choosing isn't as easy as it sounds. Why not get your friends to choose too and compare your answers?

Would you rather ...

Go ice-skating with Louis? Be his manager for the day?

Spend a day go-karting with Niall? Be taken on a personal tour of his hometown?

Go clothes shopping with Zayn? Take him to a glitzy ball?

Be Harry's hairstylist? 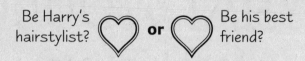 **or** Be his best friend?

Go to a restaurant with Liam? **or** Go to the movies with him?

Listen to Louis' jokes? **or** Interview him?

Go to a soccer game with Niall? **or** Appear in the band's new music video?

Take a helicopter ride with Zayn? **or** Let him cook you his fave meal?

Be Louis' makeup artist? 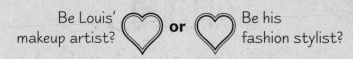 or Be his fashion stylist?

Sing a duet with Liam? 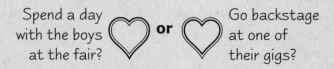 or Have him sing a song to you?

Spend a day with the boys at the fair? ♥ or ♥ Go backstage at one of their gigs?

Have Harry write a song for you? ☆ or ☆ Have him come to visit you at home?

Be the boys' singing coach? ♥ or ♥ Be their personal trainer?

RIGHT DIRECTION

See how quickly you can put the answers to these clues into the crossword on the opposite page. The answers can be found on page 95.

Across
3. Zayn was born in this month (7)
4. The band member whose older brother is called Greg (5)
5. Liam's birthday is in this month (6)

Down
1. "What makes you _____" (9)
2. Member of the band who refused to dance at Bootcamp (4)
3. Michael _____ , one of Harry's musical idols (7)

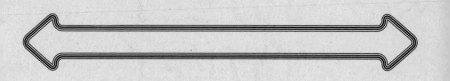

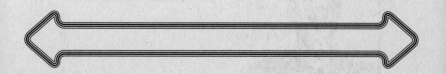

TWEET TWEET

Who is this mystery tweeter? Read the tweets below and write who you think it is at the bottom of the page. See if you were right by checking page 95.

🐦 *Being on radio is fun*

🐦 *Na na na na na naa na na na na na na naaa :p*

🐦 *just want to say a massive thank you to all our uk fans who came to the tour you made our first tour very special*

🐦 *If you are outside the tour bus can you shout I love cheese?*

🐦 *Well that was embarrassing.just been caught talking to myself and shadow boxing lol*

The mystery tweeter is ...

Answer.............................

THE FACT FACTOR:
♡ ZAYN ♡

Here are four facts and one fib about ZAYN MALIK.
Put a check in the circle beside each statement that you
think is true and a cross if you think it's a lie.

1. Zayn is from Guildford in Surrey, England.

2. Before *The X Factor*, Zayn planned to go to college to study English and become a teacher.

3. If he could be an animal, he would most like to be a lion.

4. Zayn's fave boy band is *NSYNC.

5. The only musical instrument Zayn can play is the triangle.

Answers on page 95.

!VIDEO STARS!

One of the group's favorite things about being in a band is getting to shoot cool music videos in lots of different locations.

In each of One Direction's music vids, you can tell how much fun they're all having, but how much do you know about the videos and the shoots that created them? Read the statements below and see if you can figure out which video each one is referring to. You can find the answers on page 95.

1. During this shoot, Louis got pulled over by the police ... for driving too slowly!

2. For this video, the boys visited London's Covent Garden and Trafalgar Square.

3. Zayn got to kiss a gorgeous girl at the end of this video.

4. Three words: Big. Red. Bus.

....

5. The lucky boys flew to L.A. to shoot this video.

....

6. Harry confessed to falling a little bit in love with one of the girls on this video shoot.

....

7. This video includes Zayn on a train and Harry on a moped.

....

8. This video features lots of One Direction's fans, showing their love for the fab five.

....

FAN MANIA

Can you circle the word that correctly completes each quote from the One Direction boys? Check to see if you got them all right on page 95.

1. LIAM: "Harry's the favorite with the fans. It's not upsetting. It's sort of typical because he's the _____."

cheekiest   youngest   cutest

2. NIALL: "It's mad. There are _____ everywhere we go calling out our names. They're camped outside the house and outside the studio and they stay there for hours."

girls   photographers   journalists

3. HARRY: "Any 16- or 17-year-old lad is going to enjoy _____, so I think it's nice to have."

female attention   fame and fortune
this experience

4. LIAM: "We have the best _____ ever."

moms   dance moves   fans

SEARCH FOR A STAR

Dream of some stardom for yourself? Try this quiz to see if you have what it takes to enter *The X Factor* and impress the judges. Write your answer to each question in the stars. Then turn to page 87 to see your star potential.

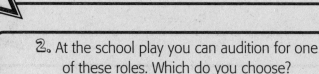

1. At a party, what are you most likely to do?

a. Take center stage on the dance floor for most of the evening.
b. Play it cool by only getting up to dance when the best songs are played.
c. Make a beeline for the best-looking person in the room.

2. At the school play you can audition for one of these roles. Which do you choose?

a. The lead role—even though the character is a little dull.
b. The much more interesting supporting role.
c. The funniest role that will get the biggest laughs.

3. It's your birthday! What is at the top of your wish list?

a. Enrollment at an acting school.
b. A new MP3 player.
c. A karaoke machine.

4. You get to meet one of the boys from One Direction. What do you say?

a. Tell him that you, too, are going to be a star—in fact, you'll be bigger than him!
b. Ask him for some career advice.
c. Gush about what a big fan you are.

5. What is your fave TV show?

a. *The X Factor.*
b. *I'm A Celebrity… Get Me Out Of Here!*
c. *Glee.*

6. On your school talent night, what do you do?

a. Sing the latest Lady Gaga hit on your own.
b. Team up with someone for a duet.
c. Form part of a group, where you each take turns to sing a verse.

7. What would you most like to do?

a. Host your own *The X Factor*-style talent competition and invite all your friends to attend.
b. Take music and singing lessons—you'd love to read music and have a pitch-perfect voice.
c. Go to your fave group's gig—watching live performances is the best.

8. How would your friends describe you?

a. Starry-eyed.
b. Cool and trendy.
c. A great laugh.

9. Your local newspaper heard about your performance in a talent competition and wants to interview you. How do you react?

a. Spend all weekend shopping for a new outfit.
b. Just wear what you are comfortable in and instead use the time to prepare some answers to their questions.
c. Call all of your friends to tell them how excited you are.

10. Which vacation would you prefer?

a. Designer shopping and a super-posh hotel.
b. A private chalet, tucked away
in a mountain resort.
c. Pool and beach party fun in Spain.

11. Which words below are most likely
to appear on your school report?

a. Over-excited.
b. A good listener.
c. The class joker.

12. You win an award for your best academic subject.
What do you do when you accept the award?

a. Tearfully thank your family, friends, fans and
everyone who voted for you.
b. Say thank you and then congratulate the
runners-up.
c. Giggle and wave to all your friends
in the audience.

13. What kind of movie would you choose to see?

a. A musical movie.
b. A romcom.
c. An action movie.

STAR STATUS

Count up the number of As, Bs, and Cs you chose and note which letter you chose the most. Now check out your star status by reading the full analysis below.

MOSTLY As

Wow! There's nowhere you'd rather be than center stage with the spotlight fully on you. There's no doubt you have the drive and confidence to succeed and you're not about to let anyone stand in your way. Just be careful that your determination doesn't come across as pushy. Play your cards right and you may even win *The X Factor* next year. Good luck!

MOSTLY Bs

You have talent and a quiet confidence in yourself and your abilities. It takes nerve and a strong character to do what you believe in and not just follow the latest trends. Just make sure that you don't try too hard to be "cool" and forget that an audience likes to be entertained.

MOSTLY Cs

It's all about having fun as far as you're concerned. Sure, you have dreams of stardom—who doesn't? You may even get to the top, but it's not everything to you. The most important thing is to enjoy life, whatever you're doing.

HEADS IN THE CLOUDS?

With all the success, exposure, and fans wanting more and more of them, there's a danger that the boys' egos *might* get a little inflated. So how are they coping? Have they got their feet on the ground or are their heads in the clouds? You be the judge by reading the quotes and then checking either "Ground" or "Clouds."

---

1. LOUIS: "It's our aim to constantly improve. We're trying to get better each week and hopefully people at home can see that."

GROUND ◯ ◯ CLOUDS

---

2. LIAM: "I was worried about my hair straight away. They just styled it wrong. So I got on the phone to Simon and said, "I'm not happy with this," and they changed it straight away."

GROUND ◯ ◯ CLOUDS

3. HARRY: "It's always very flattering, the attention from all these girls. You can't not enjoy it—but it's a bit of a curse for me, if I'm honest."

GROUND ◯   ◯ CLOUDS

4. NIALL: "I've been compared to Justin Bieber a few times, and it's not a bad comparison. I'm here to be the best artist I can be in the world."

GROUND ◯   ◯ CLOUDS

5. LIAM: "(Girls) might become a temptation, but while we're here we've just got to keep our heads on and work."

GROUND ◯   ◯ CLOUDS

6. ZAYN: "For us, I think it was a big thing of being in the right place at the right time. I mean we know we're talented and we work hard but it's really about the timing."

GROUND ◯   ◯ CLOUDS

TWEET TWEET

Can you guess which member of One Direction posted the following Twitter tweets—Niall, Liam, Louis, Zayn, or Harry? Check your answer on page 95.

Finding a Ham and Cheese Sandwich with a good Ham to Cheese ratio is always tricky..

Spiffing Morning!!! Somehow slept on my nose and now it looks wonky[1]...

#ThisChristmas I will buy all my friends extension cables...

Work Hard. Play Hard. Be Kind.

Day of tour rehearsals today! Last night at the O2 was amazing...I quite fancy[2] a satsuma[3].

The mystery tweeter is ...

Answer.................................

---

[1] *wonky* is a British term for odd.
[2] *fancy* is a British term for want or like.
[3] A *satsuma* is a citrus fruit similar to an orange.

ALL THE ANSWERS

R U Their No. 1 Fan? (pages 6 to 8)

1. c	**5.** c	**9.** a	**13.** a
2. b	**6.** a	**10.** b	**14.** c
3. a	**7.** a	**11.** b	**15.** b
4. b	**8.** b	**12.** a	

The Fact Factor: Harry (page 9)

The fib was statement number 2.

All Directions (pages 10 to 11)

```
T A D S H S O R B S G S A H C
T F A C X L L Y M A O D R A L
H H I A Z E L H A X O E F R L
E R U F Y E H S O U R N W R E
X S Y P P D G I E H Y A E Y W
F O C E A M R W F A E Q S W O
A U S L D I I I Z G F U A P C
C P A D A V L E S K H H L A N
T G N I H T E N O W J G L B O
O O B T K O K U I O W D S C M
R N E G F L Y T H G X E I D I
F F F Z Q H Z H Y P H E U L S
D A X S L I A M R L N T O O E
A L R A C L I U K M O M U Y T
J L S T O U P P N A D U G Z A
```

Memory Games (pages 12 to 14)

1. "Kids In America"

2. Belle Amie, Diva Fever, F.Y.D.

3. Harry

4. Dannii Minogue

5. Cheryl Cole

6. "Isn't She Lovely?"

7. Niall

8. Zayn

9. "Total Eclipse Of The Heart"

10. Louis Walsh

11. Harry

12. Cheryl Cole

Secret Crushes (pages 19 to 20)

1. Louis	**3.** Zayn	**5.** Niall	**7.** Niall
2. Liam	**4.** Harry	**6.** Harry	

Lucky Numbers (page 21)

1. 13

2. 1

3. 3

4. 10

5. 14

6. 2

What Are The Chances? (pages 22 to 24)

1. True

2. False

3. False

4. False

5. True

6. True

7. False

8. False

9. True

10. False

11. True

12. False

13. True

14. False

15. False

Tweet Tweet (page 25) The mystery tweeter is Louis.

Total Trivia (pages 30 to 32)

1. Zayn

2. Harry

3. Zayn

4. Liam

5. Harry

6. c

7. b

8. c

9. c

10. b

11. b

12. a

The Fact Factor: Liam (page 33)

The fib was statement number 3.

Crisscrossed (pages 34 to 35)

Bad Boys? (pages 40 to 41)

1. Simon Cowell   **5.** Zayn
2. Louis   **6.** Louis
3. Harry   **7.** Harry
4. Niall

Spot The Difference (Picture Section)

1. The black stripe on Niall's shirt is missing in the bottom picture.
2. Niall's jacket pocket is green instead of black.
3. The stripes are missing on Louis' top.
4. Harry's belt is missing.
5. Zayn has gold buttons added to his jacket.
6. Liam isn't wearing a poppy.

Tweet Tweet (page 42) The answer is Zayn.

The Fact Factor: Niall (page 43)

The fib was statement number 1.

It's All Talk (pages 44 to 45)

1. Harry   **4.** Louis
2. Zayn   **5.** Niall
3. Liam

Which Direction? (pages 52 to 53)

A	W	L	C	X	T	R	A	F	A	C	T	O	R	A
S	S	M	A	I	L	L	I	W	E	I	B	B	O	R
F	B	R	I	T	C	D	A	P	I	C	H	N	O	G
S	X	D	D	E	A	V	C	N	G	U	L	L	J	A
C	T	I	U	O	Y	E	B	A	T	T	O	G	N	M
H	R	R	A	C	B	F	W	N	L	E	F	O	X	G
E	O	E	K	P	U	H	Y	A	S	O	T	Y	I	P
R	P	C	I	K	S	T	C	N	N	O	Y	M	L
Y	O	T	S	W	O	P	E	A	E	B	K	Y	S	G
L	O	I	S	F	H	T	I	R	A	F	W	I	L	M
C	N	O	C	E	S	B	W	Q	L	Y	T	H	J	I
O	W	N	E	G	C	O	O	U	G	H	L	L	T	X
L	T	E	B	P	R	R	A	I	D	O	E	D	I	V
E	F	R	A	L	T	S	T	N	E	M	O	M	L	F
A	L	S	D	T	O	W	G	H	O	O	Y	P	A	O

Celeb Factor (pages 54 to 55)

1. Mark Feehily
2. Joe McElderry
3. Leigh-Anne Pinnock
4. Nathan Sykes
5. Emma Watson
6. Dermot O'Leary
7. Danny Jones
8. Robbie Williams

Tour Time (pages 56 to 57)

Covers

A. "Nobody Knows"
B. "Only Girl In The World"
C. "Torn"
D. "Your Song"

Original Songs

1. "Taken"
2. "Gotta Be You"
3. "What Makes You Beautiful"
4. "Up All Night"
5. "Tell Me A Lie"
6. "I Should Have Kissed You"
7. "One Thing"
8. "Save You Tonight"

Tweet Tweet (page 58) The mystery tweeter is Niall.

The Fact Factor: Louis (page 59)

The fib was statement number 4.

Forever Or A Day? (pages 60 to 63)

1. a
2. b
3. c
4. a
5. c
6. c
7. b
8. c
9. a
10. a
11. b
12. b
13. c
14. c
15. b

0 – 5	6 – 9	10 – 15
Part-Time Fan	*Loyal Fan*	*Life-Long Fan*
You prefer to let their music do the talking rather than feeling you need to know everything about them.	You know your stuff, and obviously read as much about them as you can, as well as watching them perform. Very well done.	There's no doubt about it—you are so close to the boys that you probably know more about them than they do themselves. Amazing!

Shhh ... (pages 70 to 72)
1. Liam   **4.** Zayn   **7.** Louis
2. Zayn   **5.** Harry   **8.** Harry
3. Niall   **6.** Louis   **9.** Louis

Right Direction (pages 76 to 77)

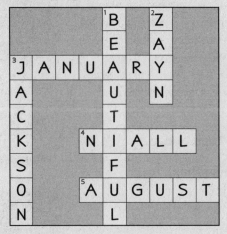

Tweet Tweet (page 78) The mystery tweeter is Liam.

The Fact Factor: Zayn (page 79)
The fib was statement number 1.

Video Stars (pages 80 to 81)
1. What Makes You Beautiful   **5.** What Makes You Beautiful
2. One Thing   **6.** What Makes You Beautiful
3. Gotta Be You   **7.** Gotta Be You
4. One Thing   **8.** One Thing

Fan Mania (page 82)
1. Youngest
2. Girls
3. Female attention
4. Fans

Tweet Tweet (page 90) The mystery tweeter is Harry.

Welcome to Justin Bieber's World

Justin Bieber: Test Your Super-Fan Status

by Gabrielle Reyes, designed by Zoe Quayle

Call yourself a Justin Bieber fan? Prove it by testing your Bieber-IQ with this book of puzzles, quizzes, and trivia questions that sum up his likes, dislikes, favorite activities, and amazing career. Pick up a pencil, solve puzzles, check your answers at the back of the book, and compare your Bieber-IQ with your friends. Includes eight pages of super color photos. (Ages 8 and older)

Paperback, 96 pp. plus 8 page color photo insert
ISBN 978-0-7641-4735-7, $6.99, *Can$8.50*

Justin Bieber Unleashed!

by Elise Munier

Here's superstar Justin Bieber's illustrated life story—and his rise to stardom as a worldwide singing sensation.

* Take a behind-the-scenes tour of his personal life and career.
* Discover what Justin is up to, on stage and off.

Packed with gorgeous color photos, personal facts about Justin's favorite things, cool quotations, and test-yourself quizzes. (Ages 8 and older)

Hardcover, 64 pp., ISBN 978-0-7641-6493-4, $7.99
Not available in Canada

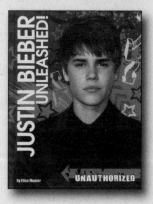

To order — Available at your local book store or visit **www.barronseduc.com**

Barron's Educational Series, Inc.
250 Wireless Blvd.
Hauppauge, N.Y. 11788
Order toll-free: 1-800-645-3476

In Canada:
Georgetown Book Warehouse
34 Armstrong Ave.
Georgetown, Ontario L7G 4R9
Canadian orders: 1-800-247-7160

Prices subject to change without notice.

(#253) R4/12